SLIDE, CHARLIE BROWN! SLIDE!

VOL. II from IT'S A DOG'S LIFE, CHARLIE BROWN!

Charles M. Schulz

CORONET BOOKS
Hodder Fawcett Ltd., London

Copyright © 1960, 1961, 1962 by United
Feature Syndicate, Inc.
First published by Holt, Reinhart and
Winston, Inc.
First Fawcett Crest printing 1968
Coronet Edition 1969
Second Impression 1969
Third Impression 1970
Fourth Impression 1971
Fifth Impression 1973
Sixth Impression 1974
Seventh Impression 1975

───────────────────────────

Printed and bound in Great Britain for
Coronet Books,
Hodder Fawcett Ltd,
St. Paul's House, Warwick Lane,
London, EC4P 4AH
by Hazell Watson & Viney Ltd,
Aylesbury, Bucks

ISBN 340 0 04407 1

YOU? YOU ADMIT YOU WERE WRONG? YOU? YOU?!

OF COURSE, CHARLIE BROWN.. AND I'LL ADMIT THAT I'VE BEEN WRONG BEFORE...

I REMEMBER THE LAST TIME I WAS WRONG ABOUT SOMETHING.. IT WAS IN 1958, I THINK... ALONG IN JULY SOMETIME, OR WAS IT IN AUGUST? YES!

THE LAST TIME I WAS WRONG WAS IN AUGUST, 1958.. I THINK IT WAS ON A MONDAY, AND...

OH, GOOD GRIEF!

I WOULD NEVER THINK OF STEALING COOKIES FROM A STORE!

NO, NEITHER WOULD I!

BUT FROM HOME... THAT'S DIFFERENT..

OH, YES, IT'S PERFECTLY ALL RIGHT TO STEAL THEM FROM YOUR MOTHER AT HOME

THAT'S WHAT IS KNOWN AS A DOUBLE STANDARD OF MORALITY!

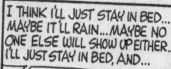

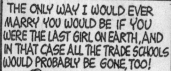

PUNT!

I HAD NO IDEA
THAT PUNTING COULD BE
SO SOUL-SATISFYING!

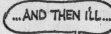

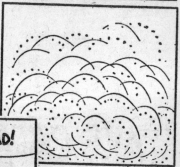

WHAT IN THE WORLD IS SO GREAT ABOUT HAVING A LIBRARY CARD?

IT'S WHAT IT STANDS FOR! THEY TRUST ME! THEY'RE HONORING MY DESIRE FOR KNOWLEDGE WITH THEIR TRUST!

IN RETURN I'M SHOWING MY FAITH IN THEIR LIBRARY BY READING THEIR BOOKS...IT'S A COMMON BOND OF TRUST...

YOU HAVEN'T GOT A LIBRARY CARD...YOU'VE GOT A **TREATY**!

YOU'D BETTER PITCH THIS NEXT GUY SOMETHING PRETTY TRICKY CHARLIE BROWN..

I'D LIKE TO SEE YOU THROW HIM AN "EXPECTORATE BALL," BUT I GUESS YOU CAN'T

THEY'VE BANNED THE "EXPECTORATE BALL" SO THERE'S NO SENSE IN EVEN TALKING ABOUT IT!

IF YOU STAND ON A PITCHER'S MOUND LONG ENOUGH, YOU MEET A LOT OF STRANGE PEOPLE!

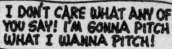

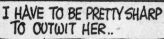

LINUS, WHY DON'T YOU PUT AWAY THAT BLANKET WHILE GRAMMA'S HERE?

YOU COULD JUST PRETEND TO GIVE IT UP, AND SHE'D NEVER KNOW THE DIFFERENCE....

BECAUSE I DON'T FEEL IT WOULD BE GOOD FOR HER TO HAVE HER OWN WAY....

HOW DO YOU EXPECT HER EVER TO BECOME MATURE?

SEE? SOMEONE'S BEEN KICKING A FOOTBALL HERE..

YOU CAN SEE HIS TRACKS IN THE NEW-FALLEN SNOW... HE'S BEEN KICKING IT ALL OVER THE YARD... BACK AND FORTH!

AND THEN HE **LEFT**! AND HE HEADED IN **THIS** DIRECTION! IF WE FOLLOW THESE TRACKS, WE RUN RIGHT INTO THE...

..."MAD PUNTER"